These Broken Creatures

Allison Manley

BookLeaf Publishing

India | USA | UK

Presentation by *BookLeaf Publishing*

Web: www.bookleafpub.com

E-mail: info@bookleafpub.com

ISBN: 9789357611695

First edition 2022

DEDICATION

This book is dedicated to me, because I deserve this shit. Also to me for being the biggest contributor to my depression—without which I could never have written these poems.

Additionally, I would like to thank my family, friends and all of the teachers who have supported me.

PREFACE

Midnight calls me to my desk. I'm impatient,
there's something sitting on the tip of my pen—I
need to write about it.

I spent the better part of 2 am chasing a fly out
of my bedroom
Maybe there's nothing poetic about it, but
When you're on your fourth cup of coffee,
Everything tastes like love

The sun rises and I finally sleep. Dawn is happy
to read the poems I've left for her, she misses the
stars too. She whispers, "Only sleepy fools write
like this. Only broken creatures can live like
this."

Miss Me?

You are beautiful,
Tonight
With the moon worshipping your skin

Being free is
Such a subtle sin

Would you miss me?
If I climbed up to the stars,
Would you miss me?
If I left the comfort of your arms,
Would you miss me?

I'm feeling sinful tonight
Beautiful, still
I would miss me

Small Talk

I am disinterested in small talk
Do not bother me
With mindless pleasantries
Rather,
Let us cut straight to the heart
Tell me your greatest desires,
Your darkest secrets
And let us share our fear of dying

The Best Kind of Influence

There is something about the beach
That truly strips a person down
Sculpted faces washed away
Empty words nowhere in the cut of our teeth
The sun is cruel
And the waves are harsh
And by the time the stars come out
We are all blazing smiles
And bare skin
And
Quite possibly making the worst kind of
mistakes
Under the influence of
Honest laughter
And cheap wine

Fragmented Souls

Their love was not the kind
To splinter under pressure
It was not akin to fine china
Which would shatter
With one callous word
With one wounded touch
With one solemn tear

No,

Their love was never flawless
They began broken
Something unfixable
Yet, they continue on
Loving each other's pieces
Knowing their fractured hearts must
Have made something close to a whole
And finding freedom
In their unassuming arms
And fragmented souls

She Is Poetry

Her blood is ink
And her bones lyrics
Her body is made up
Of poems too great for
Our little world to handle
Too hungry
To be satisfied by the likes of paper

Revolution, Revelation

A song sung in morning
Breathes life into promise
His smile keeps the clouds soaring
They revolve around him, around us

Eyes open wide, too wide?
Burnt away are all signs of obedience
The sun is blinding, up high
Branding him as another subject in a kingdom of
comedians

A salute to twilight
Register, as rain falls from a withered sky
The birds, break clouds, slow down in flight
Comedy is not popular. A song says hello, a king
says goodbye

He revolves around the clouds
The stars shine with a warning
Of sweet oblivion. He smiles still, keeping our
kingdom proud
A song sung in mourning

Forgotten Gods

Tell me, have you ever lived?
Have you danced upon our spinning Earth?
Have you inhaled the sea and exhaled the wind
and have you ever
Been struck by a vengeful Eros as he
Steals the words from your mind and the voice
from your throat
And leaves you gasping for sense before a
woman
Who strikes you as a goddess' double?
Have you kissed midnight and juggled the stars
and
Eaten ice cream for breakfast and waffles for
lunch and
Laughed in the face of Death knowing that he
could
Never really hurt you for you have lived and you
have loved more than he?
Or have you simply been existing, breathing
slowly and forgetting promptly
As you wait for Death to meet you at the finish
line?
My dear,
That is no life at all
Dance, and smile, and drive well over the speed
limit, and love and

Know that you will have lived
And know that you will be remembered by those
Gods who have long since been forgotten

Come Rome

The first night,
We arrived in Rome and
I was bitter at having to leave Paris
The air was hot and wet
And my hair stuck to my clothes
And my clothes stuck to my skin

Come morning,
I was in love

What Is A Battlefield But A Body?

I. Her momma told her that
Heaven didn't want her anymore

For she was a David
But not beautiful, nor bold
She was meek (yet determined)
Wet clay, ready for a mold

II. Her body was littered
With cuts that would scar
And her mind was burdened
With thousands of grounded stars
And dreams too heavy to shoulder

She felt alike to King Sisyphus
Always pushing against a boulder that
She knew would inevitably crush her
Yet evitable was her death

III. Her laughter wasn't sweet or melodious
(But then again, neither was she)
It didn't remind you of honey or
Summer days or romantic poetry

In fact, it wasn't slow like molasses at all
It was quick, sharp even

Her laughter was madness and snow
Storms and everything real

It was gunshots on a bloody field

IV. Gunshots
She remembers hearing them once but …
She's forgotten

V. She often compares herself to a soldier
For she's just shouldering
Through each and every dreary day
Hoping that once she decides to engage
The war will have been waged and
She can finally sleep

VI. Gunshots
One bullet, one gun
One last glance at the Sun

VII. For now she's just picking her battles
And she's not sure which one she fights will be
her last
Obeying orders, in formation, another one of
society's cattle

She's not sure she cares

VIII. *Heaven doesn't want her anymore
Does anybody?*

IX. Gunshots.

X. After all, what is a battlefield but a body?

Emotions Are Like Alcohol

Emotions are like alcohol
Where fear is vodka and
Love is cheap whiskey and
Anger is tequila and
Jealousy is fine wine and
Rum is a good time

You can mix them and
Match them and
You know that you should find
Rationality in a cup of water
But
You've been low on your luck and
They taste so good and
Everybody just wants to get
A little bit drunk

Today, and Then Tomorrow

I spent today thinking
About the shape of your lips
And how my heart begins sinking
Because I'm not on the other end of your kiss

Today I mulled over
Every possible facet of you
In the morning, that look in your eyes
And then, every little touch in the afternoon

I saved your laugh for the evening
Maybe I was hoping to glean
Something, so that I may move on from this
sorrow
But, for now, of you I'll dream

And continue my mourning tomorrow

Sylvie

Maybe,
Sylvie had been right
The whole time
And
We were just fools
Waiting for the world
To end
So,
Let us lose ourselves
Between the sheets
Happy to be alone
Content
To be forgotten to history
As the comet
Strikes home

Do You Love Him?

Her friends asked her, "Do you love him?" But
she just smiled and shook her head.
"I like the way he talks and dances, but I do not
love him yet."

Her mother asked then, "Do you love him?" And
she sighed and looked away.
"I love the way he laughs and kisses, but I'm not
sure. I couldn't say."

And then he asked her, "Do you love me?" And
she cried a little bit.
Because he's afraid of love and
She's afraid of falling and
They're both too terrified to commit.

But she knows that she does, every time she sees
him smile.
(Oh, what a wonderful mess.)
Every time he lays his head down in her lap.
And she doesn't care that it feels hopeless
As her brittle heart begins to crack.

But he's looking at her, still so scared.
So she whispers,

"How could I? When you could never love me back?"

Tell Me What Is Mine

23

They tell me to move on
That my heart will be just fine
But how can I let go of
What was never even mine?

And the World Keeps on Spinning

October reaches for me, tendrils of a haunting
memory
He whispers of masquerades and deception
He lingers like a ghost, with his falling leaves
and broken trees
He was my only exception
But I push back, no,
Let October continue dying

January clings to my skin, wipes away the tears.
Why am I still crying?
Promise to pull me back from the brink of ruin
It's a new thing, they are unfamiliar with love
but
They can offer comfort, a warm embrace, a
shelter from the snowstorm
That is my mind. The snowstorm threatening to
upturn my life
I think I could love January back

Then March dances for me, temptation in the
form of a jealous mistress
I'd have to run now, to escape her torrential rain
But I catch sight of her blooming flowers and
I'm hooked

An addict, I never stood a chance and she
beckons me
I won't be comfortable anymore, as I step into
the winds of her passionate kiss
But then, I've always been good at change, bad
at staying
Let March lead the way

Cigarettes

You, I realized far too late,
Were never the smoke left over
From a burnt out cigarette
But rather
The nicotine eating away at my lungs

I can't breathe

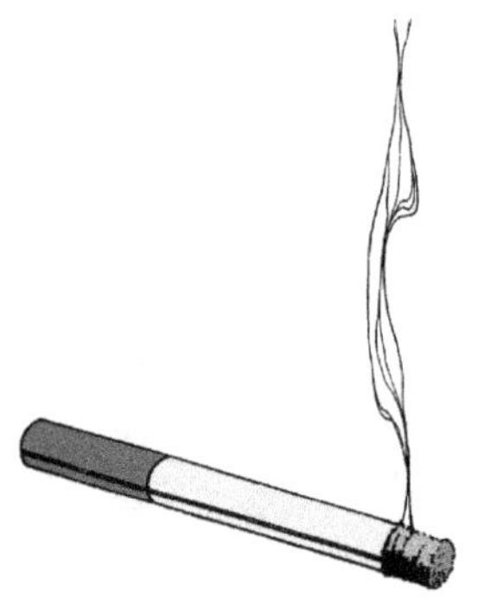

My Bucket List

I'm looking at you,
Biting back the
Wild words
Perched delicately on my lips

You're telling me of all
The things that you'll do but
I'm too focused on holding it in

"Fuck it,"
Oops, the words slipped
And I met you
In a possessive sort of kiss

We could never be just friends
Not with my hands in your hair
And
- You must have known -
You've always been on my list

Transcendence

I have these brief moments of exposure
Of air-stealing, heart-gripping transcendence
Where my soul rises above my body
And, just for a second, I see the world through a
poet's eyes

The Color Of Wild

You asked me once
What my favorite color was
And I wasn't quite sure
What to say because
Most people want a one word answer

Should I tell you that it's red?
The color of the battlefield
After all the soldiers bled?
The color that coats
Arizona's towering rocks
That incites anger and passions
Where the brain's ship of ration docks

Or maybe I'll say it's brown
Like the marshmallows that you're toasting
Or the coffee that you're roasting
Or the wrinkled pages of the books
That couldn't stand against Time's trial
Brown, the color heard in the wisdom
Hidden beyond her smile

But not to forget blue
Alike to the oceans and skies
To the teardrops that hit your pillow until the
Sun's rise

The kind of blue that reminds you
Of the waves crashing in her eyes
Which have always been far too intimate
Yes, yes I think I'll say blue
For, with blue, you are infinite

Though how can I ignore green?
The color of the forest and its tumbling leaves
Of moss, and flowers, and mint chip ice cream
It's color of the grass that will one day house
your body
And the earth that gave life to everybody

And yet still, there's orange
The color of Halloween and campfires
Of Tic Tacs, and tigers, and
Of long sunsets that inspire
And the yellow of the burning Sun
Of hot summers with a water gun
A stench named "Happy" in the air
The color that shines like gold
When woven through her hair

No, no none of these will do
Because my favorite color comes
Only in the morning dew
The color of bare skin and holy water
Of every lie and every truth
I see it in all of the "Hellos",

"Goodbyes", and "I Love Yous"

It's the color you hear
Within the beat of a heart
You can taste it when you laugh on the monkey
bars
And every time you count the stars
Or when you're driving too fast and hit a speed
bump
It's the color you feel when you're looking over
The edge of a cliff, and about to jump

I see this color everywhere
It's in every crooked smile meant
To make you laugh, right
That's only half right
Because my favorite color
Is not defined by a word

But a collision of experiences
Meant only to be felt. To be heard
My favorite color is in every child
Every adventure, memory, and possession
It is the color of all things wild

Does that answer your question?

If There Is One Thing I Have Learned

The sound of crickets
And the sight of stars
Is the quickest cure
To a racing heart

A Broken Creature Such as I

Perhaps
Gentle Aphrodite is not so gentle after all
As she dances across this battlefield as if
It were a simple stream and not
Our lives, and our souls and our minds
Oh,
Deathless daughter of the sea,
Have mercy on my heart
Let me not be overcome, once more,
With such a maddening love that
I am rendered useless,
A babbling brook of a mind
Savage Aphrodite,
You have ruined me always
I should have been prepared
It has forever been the nature of the gods
To see a broken creature such as I
And remain unmoved